southwest

To the Memory of
Ed Abbey   Bob Bundy   Tony Von Isser

and left the vivid air signed with their honor

---

southwest
Three Definitions

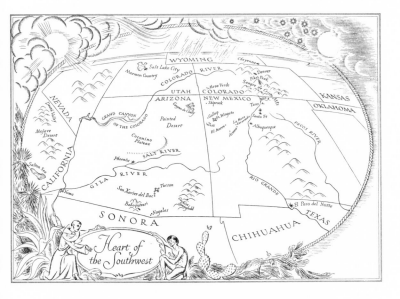

BY LAWRENCE CLARK POWELL

SINGING WIND BOOKSHOP
1990

CONTENTS

PREFACE

Throughout my life as a writer I have kept defining the Southwest and its special characteristics. Gathered here for the first time are three efforts which are harmonious, although written years apart and under differing circumstances.

Delimiting the region was easier to do. The artist, William Bellin, did it beautifully in the decorative map reproduced herewith. As a member of my UCLA Library staff he drew this map for *Heart of the Southwest*, my bibliography of novels published in 1955 by Glen Dawson.

"Arizona's Deserts" appeared originally as *Desert Splendor*, published by *Arizona Highways* in 1977, a "coffee table" book of gorgeous photographs of the quality which has made the magazine world-famous. It was this writer's hope that photographs would be chosen to illustrate the text. Alas, this did not occur. Instead their splendor put the words in the shade. This reissue of the words alone comes from the hope that they will gain meaning from not being in such competition.

In the thirteen years since *Desert Splendor* appeared there have been only superficial changes in these desert lands. Urban areas have continued to spread as Arizona remains one of our fastest growing states. Water is as ever the essential element for growth and survival. Man goes where water flows or is pumped. The Central Arizona Project now canals water overland to the valleys of the Salt and Santa Cruz rivers. An Arizona Ground Water Management Act shows new awareness of the threats to this natural resource, and yet Arizonans continue to ignore the lesson of other desert civilizations which flourished and fell. Their vestiges are seen in the valleys of the Salt and the Gila.

Whereas smelter smoke was formerly the major air pollutant, our rising use of petroleum products for transportation and generation of power has now become the worst offender. Yet Arizona's deserts remain beautiful despite destructive off-road vehicles and military exercises on the ground and in the air.

Time passes slowly in these mostly deserted lands. Although the mountains continue to be brought down by the wind and the rain, their wear is apparent only to geologists. Eventually the land's heartbreaking beauty will be here when there is no longer any heart to break for it. Yet there is no certainty that the earth will always be here. We remember the poet's prediction of ultimate dissolution for "the great globe itself, yea, all which it inherit."

To reflect on the nature and meaning of these arid lands of the Southwest is my intention. In the beginning was the word. Photographs are evanescent copies of a world which moves constantly through light and shade. Not all readers agree with the Chinese saying that one picture is worth a thousand words. Such a reader is this writer who believes that the word will also be here at the end.

These three definitions were written when sensing and saying were at maximum, as feeling and language incandesced and did not melt. If I were to be remembered, let it be for this prose. Although celebratory, it is also elegiac, as I reflect on landscapes threatened with loss. Some reassurance comes from knowing that the land will outlast its possessors as it always has. And so I end on a note of thanks and good cheer.

L. C. P.

Tucson
Bajada of the
Santa Catalinas

1

ARIZONA'S DESERTS

Visitors to Arizona see that the colors of the earth and sky differ from those back home. Greens are darker, reds more intense. The sky is bluer by day and blacker when diamonded with stars. The first sight of the desert often repels the viewer. It looks like a wasteland of scant vegetation, scattered with buttes and mesas, and veined by streambeds with more sand than water. If they have a notion of what a desert should look like, it is more apt to be from pictures of the Sahara and its sandy dunes.

Arizona's deserts are different, with their own beauty and power to hold those who take a longer look. The difference is the result of rainfall that may come in a flood or barely come at all. Yet it is sufficient to maintain the life that dwells here, including plant and animal. Whatever form life takes, to live it must acknowledge the desert's basic laws of abstinence and adaptation and prove able to survive on little.

Arizona has several deserts. There is the nearly barren Painted Desert in the north, the creosote lands of the farthest southwest, and the arboreal desert in which Tucson is situated. Aridity is what they all have in common.

1

Nowhere is there enough dependable rainfall to make Arizona uniformly green, except in such places as the great Ponderosa pine forest which surrounds Flagstaff and the conifer-clad high mountains.

Once a person becomes accustomed to Arizona's varied configurations and chromatics, the lush lands of greater rainfall, with mountains hardly more than hills, seem monotonous and sometimes smothering. A homesick Arizonan heading west in summer, beaconed by great landmark mountains, feels a reassuring sense of place when the Rio Grande is crossed and the heat is fierce and the distance far.

The cycles of human cultures in Arizona have been determined by the landscape and climate of these areas. In them water is the master element. Where there is water, even a little, life remains constant. In the north a long drought in the 13th century — tree-ring dating tells us that it lasted for 30 years — ended the culture of the cliff-dwellers called the Anasazi. Their abandoned rock-homes are found at Keet Seel, Betatakin, Canyon de Chelly and elsewhere. In the lower desert scant rainfall compelled an austere life-style for the inhabitants. We moderns have yet to learn that austerity and contentment are not incompatible.

During the past 100 years and more, as the Americans settled the Southwest, their view of the desert changed. The first emigrants found it only an obstacle on their way west. In summer they burned, in winter they froze. Water was always scarce. Dry riverbeds were the only roads. There were thorns and snakes and, most frightening of all, Apaches who regarded trespassing wagon trains as fair game.

The lure of California, where gold was said to lie in lumps for the gathering, kept the hordes on the move. The Arizona desert was no place to linger. A few prospectors, trappers and cattlemen tempted by grass along the streams, were exceptions. For years none could successfully compete with the Apaches.

But upon the advent of the 20th century, the Americans came to view the desert in a different light. The Apaches had been restrained. Reclamation brought agriculture, the automobile diminished distance. Electricity made desert life possible the year around. Cities arose as people came to live, work and play in the sun and shade. The desert became a perennial paradise.

Our changing view of the desert includes a rising concern for its preservation from overuse, heralded in 1901 by a book called simply *The Desert*. Its author, John C. Van Dyke, was an eastern art critic — although he was no tenderfoot — who came to the arid lands for his health and out of curiosity. He adapted to the climate by dressing as the Mexicans and Indians did, in cotton drawers and shirt, moccasins and straw hat. With a tough little Indian horse and a fox terrier for his only company, Van Dyke ventured deep into the tripartite southwestern desert — Mojave, Colorado, Sonora — across the Colorado River and up its tributary, the Gila, from Yuma to Gila Bend, and on to Casa Grande, Tucson and down into Sonora, traveling light and depending upon uncertain springs and waterholes, all the time accumulating facts and absorbing impressions for his book.

"It was written," he recalled years later, "during that first summer (1898), at odd intervals when I lay with my back against a rock or propped up in the sand. That was a summer of strange wanderings. The memory of them comes back to me now mingled with half-obliterated impressions of white light, lilac air, and heliotrope mountains and blue sky. I cannot well remember the exact route of the odyssey, for I kept no record of my movements. I was not traveling by map. I was wandering for health and desert information."

The Desert was followed by many books by other writers on the desert. Yet it was the first to perceive and to praise the arid lands as both beautiful and precious. Van Dyke accurately described the plant and animal life, the configurations and climate. He saw the importance of adapting to and not trying to change the desert. He had none of the comforts that have enabled us to master the desert — or at least to suffer the illusion that we have done so.

4

Lessons of adaptation can be learned from Arizona's Indians. The Papagos are prime examples, at least historically, of living not unhappily on little. Of all the tribes, they have always had the least water. On their reservation west-south-west of Tucson, no year-round streams flow, no copious aquifer underlies the land. The Papagos are dependent upon winter rains from the Pacific for replenishing their springs and waterholes, and upon summer's thunderous flash floods from the Gulf of California for greening their cornfields.

The Papagos inhabit an arboreal desert of saguaro, ocotillo, palo verde, and mesquite. From trees and bushes they gather the fruits, beans and seeds. From native grasses they weave baskets for carrying and storing. The ribs of the saguaro and the canes of the ocotillo provide their materials for huts against the rain and ramadas for shade. They are reconciled to their land of little water. An old Papago woman once said, "To you whites, Elder Brother gave wheat and peaches and grapes. To us, he gave wild seeds and the cactus. These are the good foods."

South from the Gila River, which includes this Papago country, the arboreal desert land rises toward Mexico. Here each additional few feet of elevation means more rainfall, in short seasonal spurts. This accounts for the dark green of the area's flora, which has adapted to the cycle. When the rain falls, they gulp and store. When they have flowered, they seed and are ready for resurrection in the next rainy cycle. Their survival depends upon their swiftness. If there should be a radical change in the water, the desert would alter. More rain, greener growth, less rain, a dying back to the hardiest species.

The dictionary definition of *desert* does not apply to this land: "an uncultivated region without inhabitants; a dry, barren, region largely treeless and sandy." There is cultivation here. There have always been inhabitants, as well as trees and shrubs and scant sand.

The City of Tucson, the Old Pueblo of Spanish-Mexican times, now spreads over the Santa Cruz River valley on the eastern edge of the arboreal desert. This has long been a fertile valley because of the river, which once flowed, more or less, throughout the year. Indians have lived here for at least 15,000 years. And, here, the Spanish founded missions, presidios, and pueblos.

When the Americans came they found that Tucson lay at the crossroads from the east and up from Mexico, a natural trading center for ranchers, miners, and the military. The climate was healthful. The state university eventually lent character to the city. The clear air brought astronomers. And worldwide arid lands studies logically centered here.

The rising demands of agriculture, mining, and population gradually consumed the Santa

Cruz river's surface flow. Now pumps are called upon to tap the water beneath the valley. The balance of nature began to be altered. Today Tucson is seeking to learn how much longer it can continue to consume its water supply without replenishment. Even the completed Central Arizona Project will not meet all of the region's needs.

Tucson is a good point of departure into the surrounding desert. This region demonstrates how elevation determines vegetation. The highway up Mt. Lemmon, highest point in the Santa Catalina Mountains, rises over a mile in half an hour of easy driving, traversing the life zones from saguaro, palo verde and ocotillo through juniper and piñon to oak, pine and spruce.

Here at the 10,000-foot summit, overlooking the river-plain and city, is a coniferous and deciduous forest. In winter the snow falls and people come to ski. Together with other ranges, the Rincons, Santa Ritas, and Huachucas, the Santa Catalinas form an archipelago of desert islands.

Another way to leave the city is by the river road, south to Sonora, and past Mission San Xavier del Bac, the gleaming White Dove of the Desert. Orchards beyond Green Valley are not native. They are pecan trees that also lay claim to the underground water.

Along the border are oak-groved grasslands. The low mountains are rain-catchers. Because

7

there is never enough rain, it is still an arid land, although not a desert in the dictionary sense.

Here the Santa Cruz rises in creeks from the slopes of the Huachuca Mountains and from springs at the head of the San Rafael Valley. Along the young river's course are pools and *cienegas* where birds feed, including blue herons and belted kingfishers, as well as migratory geese and ducks.

This is a sweet land of far distance and deep silence, here at the meeting of American Arizona and Mexican Sonora. Wildlife ignores boundaries. The blueness of mountains belongs to no country. Not far to the east four centuries ago, Coronado marched along the river road of the San Pedro in his vain search for what were rumored to be cities with roofs and walls of gold.

West of the Santa Cruz and beyond the mountains lies the valley of the Altar. Less rainfall means that its mesquites are runty, its colors subdued. Much of its rain comes in summer from the south. *Arroyos* (usually dry washes) are gouged by the runoff from these savage storms.

To the west rises the guardian range of the Baboquivaris, buttressed at both ends by sacred peaks. In the south is Baboquivari Peak, revered by the Papagos as the home of the gods. It is a monolithic mountain of granite whose conical helmet is visible for 100 miles around.

At the Baboquivaris' northern end is Kitt Peak. To the National Science Foundation the Papago tribe granted the right to build thereon the great Kitt Peak National Observatory. Here "men with long eyes" revere Newton and Einstein. Whereas the summit of Baboquivari Peak can be attained only by those with strong legs and good wind, Kitt Peak is easily reached by car over a paved road.

The slopes of the Baboquivaris support a variety of wildlife, all linked in a natural food chain. Rabbits, quail and dove feed the coyotes and hawks. Cougars eat the deer. Buzzards pick the bones. During the heat of summer the silence is broken by the drumming rattle of the roadrunner in pursuit of lizard or little bird, by the monotonous croon of the Inca dove, and by the piercing cry of the Gambel's quail.

Everywhere on the Arizona desert there are mountains in sight. The arid lands are an islanded sea. From the tops of these mountains, on clear or dusty days, at dawn, noon, or sundown, the desert assumes infinite shapes and colors.

"Look out from the mountain's edge once more," Van Dyke wrote at the close of his book. "A dusk is gathering on the desert's face, and over the eastern horizon the purple shadow of the world is reaching up to the sky. The light is fading out. Plain and mesa are blurring into unknown heights. Warm drifts of lilac-blue are drawn like mists across the valleys; the yellow sands have shifted into pallid gray. The glory

9

of the wilderness has gone down with the sun. Mystery — that haunting sense of the unknown — is all that remains."

Night belongs to the coyotes. Their yap and chatter and wail are meant to start up their dozing prey. The owl hunts silently. The mountain lion screams like a woman in pain.

The night sky is incredibly luminous. Here it is apparent why Religion and Astronomy were born in the desert. Man is reduced by distance and silence to worship the arching infinite and to seek out its mystery. Only the ocean rivals the desert in this sense of immensity.

This arboreal desert land is more fragile than it appears to be. Although the saguaro, monarch of desert plants, looks invincible and lives for a century or more, it falls like a straw to the bulldozer. All the cactuses are vulnerable to man. We can be proud that Arizona leads the states in laws to protect its unique vegetation. Together with the Grand Canyon, the cactus is Arizona's greatest photogenic asset. Visitors are always amazed by the brilliant and delicate floral display of cactus in the spring.

To the Papagos the saguaro is more than a picturesque plant to be photographed against the sky. Its fruit is a source of sugar and oils. In harvesting it they employ slender poles to dislodge the fruit. The harvest is also a way of invoking the summer rains to drop their blessing on the thirsty land.

From the boiled fruit of the saguaro the Papagos make their liquor. The crimson pulp is their sweet, the seeds a source of flour and grease. Then follows the ceremony of fermentation, a gathering in the village to chants such as this one translated by the anthropologist Ruth Underhill in her book, *Singing for Power:*

> *Our fire has burned and the sun has gone*
> *   down,*
> *Come together, following our ancient custom.*
> *Sing for the liquor,*
> *Delightfully sing.*

"Until morning they sing songs of rain and cloud," she writes, "of the little red spiders and the little gray horned toads who are the friends of the rain, and of the frogs who are its messengers."

On the eastern edge of the Papago Reservation, not far from Tucson, the plant and animal life of the Sonoran Desert may be seen and studied in the Arizona-Sonora Desert Museum. This unique museum offers lessons in environment and appreciation of an essentially rich region.

Although the Colorado is Arizona's most celebrated river, as the carver of its grandest canyon, it is the Gila that is the state's ancient lifeline. Like a great snake the Gila River lies across Arizona. From the cliff dwellings of its headwaters in the mountains of the New Mexico border to the river's union with the

Colorado at Yuma, Indians have immemorially made their home along the Gila.

The Colorado's extremes of gorge and flood plain made it impossible for the tribes to establish lasting cultures in its depths or on its banks. The squash and melon farming of the Mojaves and Yumas, along the lower reaches of the river, provided only seasonal bounty that depended on variable forces up in the Rockies where the river rises.

In contrast, the Gila has long been Arizona's river of life. Its flow was less violent, its descent more gradual, its valley better suited to farming. And here man has lived in harmony with his environment.

The early Gilans were good water-engineers. They knew how to draw off the river's flow by a network of canals that irrigated lands removed from the threat of flood. Why their time came to an end we do not know. Was it a long drought that saw the Gila run dry? Did over-irrigation kill the soil with rising alkali? Or did predatory tribes come from the northeast and overthrow the peaceful river-people?

The Pima Indians, who now live along the lower Gila, call their vanished predecessors the Hohokam, meaning "those who went away or were all used up." The Casa Grande Ruins National Monument near Coolidge is evidence of the Hohokam's skill as builders. And here is also a mystery. Was it a communal building, or a temple, or an observatory?

12

In 1887 the Hemenway Expedition, led by Cushing and Hodge, first unearthed the canals and dwellings of the Hohokam. In our time the work of Gladwin and Haury has discovered their sites at Los Muertos and Pueblo Grande on the Salt and at Snaketown on the Gila.

As to the Pimas, a century ago American settlement disrupted their lives. The gold seekers had found them ready to trade squash, melons and grain for goods and trinkets. If the Pimas had any bad habits, the worst was probably their penchant for stealing untended mules.

The decline of the Pimas began when the Americans upriver from Casa Grande diverted the Gila for their own fields.

In Arizona who owns the water owns all. Nowhere is this truer than in the valley where the Gila takes tributary water from the Salt, Agua Fria, and Hassayampa. Unlike Tucson, whose water comes from pumped wells, Phoenix derives it life mostly from rivers that run in all seasons. While Tucson is using its groundwater faster than it is being replenished, Phoenix's supply is unending, at least as long as the mountains bring down the rain and the snow.

Now the completed Central Arizona Project is pumping additional water overland from the Colorado River for the Salt River Valley's urban and agricultural needs. This is a dependency not without danger. Even the mighty Colorado owes its life to snowmelt from the Rockies.

The rise of this desert Phoenix and the flowering of its valley are the result of creative hydraulics. From dams came flood control, water storage, and generated power. The barren land was made habitable and fruitful. A series of dams on the Salt and Verde culminates in Granite Reef Dam just below the two rivers' confluence. From there canals distribute water to Phoenix and the valley, even as the Hohokam did, by a network of channels to farms and people and the industries that have been drawn to this sun-drenched desert.

Flowing water had made Phoenix into an oasis. Palm trees line its straight streets. Dark groves of orange and grapefruit bear gold and yellow fruit. A civic plaza is adorned with sculptures and fountains. High buildings shine in the sun, while around the city colored flelds of vegetables, grains, and cotton ripen and cattle fatten for the market. All of this bounty came to pass in a hundred years. Water, soil, and sunshine, plus man's imaginative determination were responsible.

Water, power, and the automobile have made Arizona habitable, expansive, and mobile. Although it has been tempered, heat has not been abolished. The sun is still monarch. The desert can never be scorned nor entered carelessly. Without water and shade in summer, man cannot long survive. Air pollution now threatens Phoenix. Can man master it as he did heat?

Dams also have changed life along the banks of the Colorado River. Like the Gila River Indians, the Colorado tribes also have been affected by the white man's arrival. No longer are the margins of the stream enriched by the overflow of silt in the spring floods. Crops of squash and melons are seldom raised individually, instead the Indians of the river tribes are more apt to work in vast irrigated fields in the river valley.

The shores below the dams provide an ideal habitat for recreation and retirement. Pleasure boats abound. The summer's heat is borne with shade and cooling, but the weather can change with savage suddenness. There is no security from wind and rain and flash flooding.

At the Yuma Crossing, near where the Colorado enters Mexico, the ghosts of the past are encountered. The reflective traveller sees history as a continuum, as a pageant of time past, present, and future. The desert seems richer if we see it thus, if against the sky as the peaks turn purple and night descends, we envision the river of 200 years ago when Anza and his colonists made the crossing on their way from Sonora to northern California and the eventual founding of San Francisco. Their passage was celebrated by a feast of melons, dug up from sandy storage by the friendly Yumas.

Readers of Arizona's classic literature recall that Martha Summerhayes was here at the Yuma Crossing 100 years ago. She came with her soldier husband in the campaign to contain the Apaches. They were bound upriver to Ehrenberg and then overland to Fort Whipple. The undammed river ran high in summer so that steamers plied from the Gulf 200 miles to Fort Mojave. The troops were towed behind in open barges. When the temperature soared to 123 degrees, three of the men died from sunstroke.

Martha Summerhayes found Ehrenberg the bitter end of the world. Here is how she described it in *Vanished Arizona:* "Of all the dreary, miserable-looking settlements that one could possibly imagine, that was the worst. An unfriendly, dirty, and heaven-forsaken place." Little did she dream that her husband was destined to be posted there later for a tour of duty.

Then she came to envy the Mexican's dress style that Van Dyke wisely adopted. "Oh!" she cried, "if I could only dress as the Mexicans do! Their necks and arms do look so cool and clean. I have always been sorry I did not adopt their fashion of house apparel. Instead of that, I yielded to the prejudices of my conservative partner, and sweltered during the day in high-necked and long-sleeved white dresses, kept up the table in American fashion and ate American food in so far as we could get it. At those times, how I wished I had no silver, no table linen, no china, and could revert to the primitive customs of my neighbors."

By the time she came in old age, at home on Nantucket Island, to write her memoirs, she exemplified what thousands since have realized — that the desert works its spell and that some who first fear it, come to love it beyond all else on earth. "The desert was new to me then," she wrote. "I had not read Pierre Loti's wonderful book, *Le Desert,* and I did not see much to admire in the desolate wastelands through which we were traveling. I did not dream of the power of the desert, nor that I should ever long to see it again. But as I write, the longing possesses me, and the pictures then indelibly printed upon my mind, long forgotten amidst the scenes and events of half a lifetime, unfold themselves like a panorama before my vision and call me to come back to look upon them once more."

In our time we have reached a new awareness of the desert. Arizonans now realize that their arid lands are a priceless asset whose value lies as much in their *not* being developed as in their future exploitation, whether for industry, agriculture, cities or pleasure.

Arizona's prosperity derives abundantly from tourism. Billions of dollars are spent each year by visitors who come primarily for sun, distance, and color. And people will continue to seek the desert for the good of body and soul, for healing, history and room in which to stretch. If only for the economic benefits, we would be wise to keep the state mostly as God

17

made it. And yet we must recognize that green lawns, golf links, and swimming pools are desired by many Arizonans and are also responsible for thousands of people coming to live in the state.

Today we are taking a new look at our passion for lawns and green parks. Native gardens and natural landscaping are seen as good taste and good sense. A braking action has begun to protect our environment. Arid lands studies at the University of Arizona in Tucson and solar energy research at Arizona State University in Tempe are signs of our mounting concern.

We are going back to nature for examples of adaptation. When rain falls, the saguaro stores it in its expandable tissues and thus survives heat that dehydrates more intelligent forms of life. There is also the kangaroo rat, described by Joseph Wood Krutch, that makes its own water supply from seeds it eats. The mesquite's innate sense warns it not to leaf out until it is sure that freezing nights have passed. And there is the creosote bush that needs little water to attain great beauty — glossy-leafed, starry-flowered and strongly scented when wet by the rain.

The desert indeed teaches adaptation for survival. If we will learn, we should live long as a desert people. We are tenants, not owners, of this precious place in the sun. Tenants are transients, witness the departure of our predecessors who left deserted caves and dry canals.

What will we leave our successors? There could be no richer heritage than virgin desert. There is an innate wisdom and logic in nature. Life persists when balance is maintained. Each link in the chain of being has its meaning and importance. If the balance is broken and the chain snapped, there are the inevitable and dangerous consequences.

Newspapers, magazines, books, television, all have become wordy. We speak of the interconnectedness of the ecosystems, of the delicacy of the natural fabric, and of the fragility of the environmental web. Yet, whatever we call it, we know that life is woven and webbed into a magical garment that we rend at our peril. Balance and Being are laws which must be obeyed if we are not to suffer their breaking.

Since Van Dyke no one has better expressed concern for the preservation of desert values than Krutch. He also is another example of the unlikely convert to the desert. Not until middle age did this eastern literary critic come to reside in Arizona. Then he fell under the spell and stayed to the end of his life. In *The Desert Year* and *The Voice of the Desert,* Krutch came to fame as a philosopher-naturalist and conscience-voice of the desert.

"To those who listen," Krutch wrote, "the desert speaks of things with an emphasis quite different from that of the shore, the mountains, the valleys or the plains. Whereas they invite action and suggest limitless opportunity, exhaustless resources, the implications and the mood of the desert are something different. For one thing the desert is conservative, not radical. It is more likely to provoke awe than to invite conquest. It does not, like the plains, say, 'Only turn the sod and uncountable riches will spring up.' The heroism which it encourages is the heroism of endurance, not that of conquest."

"Precisely what other things it says depends in part upon the person listening. To the biologist it speaks first of the remarkable flexibility of living things, of the processes of adaptation which are nowhere more remarkable than in the strange devices by which plants and animals have learned to conquer heat and dryness. To the practical-minded conservationist it speaks sternly of other things, because in the desert the problems created by erosion and overexploitation are plainer and more acute than anywhere else. But to the merely contemplative it speaks of courage and endurance of a special kind."

That all of these listeners are now to be found increasingly among Arizonans leads us to hope that far into the future, all will yet be well with our most precious resource — the desert.

2

REVISTA NUEVA MEXICANA

Seek essences, enduring things, touchstones, and symbols; try to recreate in prose what makes this country so increasingly meaningful and necessary to one. Altitude, distance, color, configuration, history, and culture — in them dwell the essential things, but they must be extracted. "Crack the rock if so you list, bring to light the amethyst." Costs nothing to try. Some have succeeded — Lummis, Lawrence, Long, La Farge, Horgan, Waters, the Fergussons — proving that it is possible. Stand books on the shelf, hang up maps, gaze in the turquoise ball, finger the fragment of red adobe from Pecos, reload the blue Scripto, take a fresh yellow pad, then sit down and see what comes.

On that night in Santa Fe I read aloud from Haniel Long's unfinished book and found it good, the ripe work of a writer who waited six decades to write his first novel. This was the fourth visit in two years to Haniel and Alice Long, and again I brought offerings of tea and affection and the feather of a dove; and faintly, very faintly, I envied him his twenty-year head start and his quintessential masterpiece, published in 1936, the *Interlinear to Cabeza de Vaca*.

At dinner on a high point east of town we looked across the river valley to Los Alamos, wickedly winking with lights, while a cotton-tail nibbled grass outside the window and the flares of sunset reached the zenith.

"You can't do both," Long said. "Lead the administrative life and write."

"I'm trying. And also I want to teach. It's taken me twenty years to learn librarianship. Now I want to teach it."

"I taught for two decades at Carnegie Tech before we came here. I like to think my books continue the process."

"It was your books that brought me here. The wide world's your classroom now."

And to illustrate this, Long gave me a German translation of the *Interlinear*, to add to the French one he gave me a year ago.

Burma born, Harvard schooled, tall, lean, and gray, and suffering the same eye trouble as Huxley's, this man who founded Writers' Editions is humorous, quizzical, wise, and gentle, and I always leave him and his wife with a feeling of refreshment, redetermination, faith, and affection, and the anticipation of the riches which await a man in the decades between fifty and seventy, if he is prepared to recognize them.

The next day I entered the mission church at the Ranchos de Taos, one of the Southwest's two fairest shrines (the other being San Xavier). A party of nuns was being shown through by the priest, and they were having a jolly time, especially the youngest of the lot — a sister whose vitality, unquenched by her funereal habit, led her to peek under the red silk robe of an image to see what was beneath. I had not witnessed such spiritual vigor since Dublin.

The sundrenched fields of Taos were lush with alfalfa, goldenrod, and dandelion, exuding midsummer fragrance to the point of asphyxiation. I had been reading *The Man Who Killed the Deer*, and I wanted to see the Blue Lake of the Taoseños. The sign promised a route, but it proved to be only by trail. The road corkscrewed fifteen miles up the Arroyo Hondo, down which white water was foaming. At Twining, elevation 9,412, the road became traversible only by jeep. The air was sharp, and smoke from a campfire rose unwaveringly into an eggshell sky. The bald dome of Mt. Wheeler rose another few thousand feet higher. A trail-sign pointed to Lobo Peak, on whose aspened shoulder I had visited Frieda Lawrence in 1941.

Everywhere I went the new edition of the New Mexico State Guide was open on the seat beside me, full of facts and photos and a minimum of misleading information. I never could find the church of San Miguel del Bado as the Guide had described it, or it must have been stuccoed over what the book said was stone, but the side trip brought an even greater reward.

I had been earlier in Las Vegas, having come over the Sangres from Taos, through the Penitente villages of Picurís and Mora, traversing a high back country of few people and no people, of drizzle and shower and cloud-piled skies, past fields of corn and flowers and heavenly bluebirds, over the haunted route of Coronado, Armijo, and Los Tejanos, of Gregg and Kearny; and in the station there had seen mixed Santa Fe trains, none of which had quickened my pulse — cars, crews, passengers, all ordinary.

And then on this detour, having crossed the Pecos and reached the tiny station of Ribera, I saw a wondrous sight: the westbound Super Chief drawn up on a siding. That meant only one thing: its eastbound counterpart was due, and O Lord! there it was, coming round the turn, the long snake of silver Pullmans drawn by the monstrous red and yellow double diesel, pulling, pulling, with deep-throated, smoking exhausts, horning once for the passing, the engineer riding high on his throne, his gloved hand raised slightly in response to my enthusiastic wave, there at that orgasmic moment of midway meeting; and to crown it all, sight of an old friend, the Pullman car Coconino Princess, on which I had ridden before, coupled between Pine Meadow and Regal Junction, as fair a vision as these eyes have ever seen.

The westbound train gathered speed slowly and I lingered alongside it for several miles, its pony trucks clickety-clicking over the rail-points, until finally it pulled away from me, approaching Glorieta Pass and the descent to Lamy and Albuquerque. The engineer waved as I turned off to Pecos Pueblo, a ruin abandoned in 1838, now a state monument.

Rain began to fall again, darkening the red

soil and the green piñons, and I got soaked while dashing in and out of the ruins of the church, which is dedicated to the same lady as my home town — Nuestra Señora la Reina de los Angeles. Without planning it I found myself traversing Pecos Village and once again following a river to its headwaters, while the car radio transmitted such sentimental songs as to make me long to learn the guitar — songs with apparently no other words than *corazón, amor, alma, y mujer.* Well, what else is there? *Libros.* I had not realized that this fabled river rises in the Sangres, and I preferred the mountain aspect of the stream, lined with a Cistercian monastery and a State Fish Hatchery and the strange modern hacienda of Arnold B. Friedman, to the lower Pecos country of Billy the Kid and worse. (I learned later that this hacienda is the only work in New Mexico by Frank Lloyd Wright.)

This search for the source is a philosophical urge, as well as physiographical, a blind going upward to the beginning of things, while the world narrows in and all else is eliminated. This focus on the basic elements is purifying, therapeutic, electrifying, and this way of recharging by stripping away is a dedicatory one, well suited to this Angeleno who lives ordinarily in the midst of multiplicity. Such were my thoughts up where the Pecos rises.

East of the Sandías the road runs north to Golden and Madrid. What's in a name? Much —

especially if the name is foreign and musical. When asked for the most musical words in English, regardless of meaning, a foreigner replied "cellar door." Thus the Sandías, to one ignorant of Spanish. The Watermelon Mountains? Well, yes, as long as the mind doesn't visualize the seedy fruit.

The Sandía Mountains. How different they appear when seen from the east, dark green and wooded all the way up, humped like a whale, without the bare face they present to Albuquerqueans. Southernmost of their sacred peaks, the range was called Turtle Mountain by the Pueblos. The turnoff to the crest was alluring, but I had miles to go before I parked, and the compass pointed north. Golden? Hardly. Madrid? A company coal town, obviously misnamed. The beauty of this lonely route lay in the piñon forest, and in the clouds that were just beginning to cap the sky.

At Cerrillos I came to an unexpected crossing of the railroad, the main line of the Santa Fe, and on a hunch I turned off and cruised through the village. I stopped by a group of natives on the porch of the grocery. "Any trains due?" I asked, briskly. Whereupon one of them lurched toward me, preceded by his boozy breath. "My friend," he pronounced, "there passes here one train every half hour," and he staggered back to his fellows. They laughed, as I drove on, crossed the tracks, and reconnoitered. Not a sound or sign of life, only shining rails. Then I spied a lank sack hanging from the trackside

26

hook and a car parked alongside, with a woman sleeping in it. The mail train was due. I waited, and pretty soon heard the low hum of an approaching diesel. A full five minutes passed before it burst round the curve, heading northeast to Lamy and Las Vegas, and bore down on the station with overriding urgency. The Super Chief, no less. The sack was hooked in, and an equally thin one thrown off. The silver vision passed. Toroweap, Tierra Amarilla, Cloudcroft, but this time my Princess was coupled elsewhere. The woman got out, picked up the sack, drove off. I had witnessed the postmistress of Cerrillos at work.

I paid my first visit to the Museum on the outskirts of Santa Fe and saw an exhibition of contemporary arts and crafts of great beauty; silver and wood, turquoise and wool, the elements worked by hand with loving skill, the objects displayed in imaginative ways, to give one of the best museum experiences I have ever had.

City of the Holy Faith, huddle of abodes, cottonwooded, piñoned, ringed by ranges with ringing names: the Sangre de Cristos, the Sandías, the Jemez. Day's end and the mountains were blue black; again a lone rabbit, this time a big-eared jack, nibbling and sniffing his way across the somnolent landscape, as I looked north to the last light on Truchas, knowing that the morrow would find me on upland slopes.

The morrow was Sunday, and I saw people in their best, as once again I left the highway and took a dirt road to Chimayó and beyond, a

27

gentle climb against the flow of water, past fields and flowers and burdened orchards. "Cherries, cherries," cried the children, from where they crouched by the roadside, holding out handfuls of the little red fruit.

All the beautiful choices were mine, whether to seek the fabled *santos* in the Santuario of Chimayó or to see the Valley of Córdova, where Joseph Krumgold made *And Now Miguel*, that almost unbearably beautiful documentary film of sheepherding and a small boy's dream. One must always choose among several, and Truchas was my choice, an ancient village lying exposed on a hogback, inanimate on this Sunday morning, yet eternally alive, as the ghost towns of Arizona are not. Metals were not the reason for Truchas's naked site. The villagers built there originally for defense against their enemies, descending to the fields, or driving their sheep to mountain meadows.

I crawled along the spinal street, seeing a crocheted peacock in a window, potted geraniums everywhere, a rainbow-painted wall and matching eaves (someone was crazy for color), stacked woodpiles, and I breathed piñon smoke from cooking stoves.

Once again choice was necessary, and I bore north over piney slopes, instead of climbing higher toward the Truchas Peaks and the next highest point in New Mexico (Wheeler Peak, 13,151 feet; North Truchas Peak, 13,110 feet). I came at last to the *cor cordium* of Spanish New Mexico, the ancient village of Las Trampas. It was noon and the priest had locked the church and gone to lunch. So had everyone. The pueblo-like plaza was deserted, except for a car with Montana plates, but I could feel eyes on me as I prowled around the classic church of Santo Tomás del Rio de las Trampas, coming on a store of wooden crosses piled against the rear wall, evidence that this was indeed deep penitente country.

Leaving the village and descending toward Peñasco on the Rio Pueblo, I met a rodeo of pickup trucks and young men in white shirts, and a short distance beyond I saw a girl in a red dress disappearing through the piñons.

In Taos again was the ubiquitous smell of burning piñon, recalling Peattie's words in his book on trees: "They say that those who, like Kit Carson, had once known the bells, the women and the pinyon smoke of Taos could never stay away — come Kiowa, come Sioux, come Kansas blizzard or calabozo."

El Crepúsculo carried news of the death in San Diego of Bert Phillips, one of Taos's founding artists, and of the visit of Frieda Lawrence's daughter Barbara while Frieda's husband Angie was in Italy. I found Frieda in the house on the plain at El Prado, thanks to the directions of Joe Montoya's son at the family service station, where he was being aided by a swarm of boys, each of whom performed one automotive chore in slow motion, a pleasant change from metropolitan "minute men" service. I had not seen Frieda in five years, and found her still a fountain of friendly vitality. If Swift and Pope and the other bachelor misanthropes could have known a woman like Frieda, English literature would have been different, in the way it differed through what she gave Lawrence; and as we sat over tea and biscuits and spun the thread of talk clear back to the fateful day she first saw him in flannels and blazer and red beard, launching cockleshell boats for her children, I knew that this was basic to all literary history, that literature is made by men *and* women, a fact best understood by French critics.

South of Eagle Nest, State Highway 38 takes off to the east, giving promise, on the map, of a graded road over the mountains to Mora. The promise was not kept. What appeared on paper to be a beautiful back road was actually a deteriorating set of ruts, suited only to truck or jeep. I was driving a Chevrolet coupé, albeit a powerful eight-cylinder job, and with the automatic transmission which, contrary to popular belief, is excellent for slow driving over wretched roads, because of the uniform flow of power that can be maintained down to standstill and start again. And the car was high-bedded enough to clear the boulders; so it went, but just.

The road began alluringly enough along the adobe edges of sloping meadows. Still I had an eye on the sky. It was beginning to pile up with clouds that would break with rain before the day was ended, and I didn't want to be on 'dobe when they did.

There was no sign of life, even at the occasional ranches. The highway markers were rusted and illegible, and there was an increasing number of *trancas*, gated fences, requiring all my strength to manipulate. My eyes lifted to the blue mesa toward which the road climbed. Black Lake lay to the right, a natural *ciénaga* edged with deep grass and herds of fattening Herefords. This was the last place to turn back, but I did not know it, and pressed on ignorantly past the point of no return.

Suddenly the road narrowed and grew rockier. I drove at five miles an hour, grunting and sweating, in shorts and sneakers, thankful that my arms were stronger than my foresight, and really very happy not to be on Wilshire Boulevard. My comfort was a fresh set of tire tracks; otherwise I would not have known which choice to make when the road forked, as it did again and again.

Gaining the mesa at last I paused and looked back to the northern-most Sangres in the distance — Wheeler, Pueblo, and Lobos peaks, those bare "cloud-capp'd towers" — wondering how long I had before the rain came, and if there were *caliche* ahead, then turned my back on 'em and resumed my forward motion. The "road" rutted rockily through ponderosas and Engelmanns, then turned into a bouldered trough, down which I caromed toward what the map called Coyote Creek. It seemed to flow into the Guadalupita Valley, eventually to Mora and what, by contrast, would be civilization. This was the very opposite of the experience of seeking the headwaters of the Pecos and the Hondo: I longed to leave the headwaters, my muscles rigid under the hot flow of sweat, compelled to control my desire to hurry and beat the rain, and instead to crawl, bump, bounce, creep, and slither, holding horse-power and heartbeat in check. It had rained the day before, and the road was pooled and treacherous.

Then the trough tossed me into a clearing — a sawmill, with promise of human beings, of whom I had not seen one since Eagle Nest three hours before. It was a big establishment, with many sheds and cabins and parked trucks, and piles of trimmings. But no saw buzzed. No voice spoke. There was no stockpile of logs.

Nada. Nadie. Ninguno. En ninguna parte. The quintessence of nothingness. God, but it was eerie, like something out of Poe or Melville. I whistled. Echo answered. The tracks ended at still another fenced gate, leading to a ford over the creek. I parked and went around and faced a sign, and read, ABSOLUTELY NO TRESPASS-ING. Too late. I had already trespassed. Was this Highway 38, a public thoroughfare of the sovereign state of New Mexico, or was it a pri-vate road of the woodcutters? Had I taken a wrong turn up on the mesa?

And then I smelled and saw smoke, coming from a cabin chimney at the far end of the clearing. I trudged over spongy sawdust earth and called *Hola!* Two heads popped out of two windows, like boxed jacks, one red, one black. Grown boys, they belonged to, their mouths full of food, their eyes of astonishment.

"Where am I? I asked. "Can I get out?"

They laughed and came outdoors. El Rojo was an Anglo, El Moro, a *hijo de pais* who had stumps for hands.

"This is the sawmill of the Ortega Brothers," said Red, and Blackie added, "Where you from?"

"From Eagle Nest, Black Lake, and down the road to hell," I replied.

Again they laughed. "The worst is over," they assured me.

"Through the gate to Mora?"

"Sure, but don't be in a hurry. Those rocks are hungry."

"Where is everyone?" I asked.

"Logging. We just brought in a load and stopped for lunch."

"I have sweat the hunger out of me," I said.

"Where do you live?" they asked.

"In the City of Angels," I replied, "and I bring you blessings from Nuestra Señora."

They crossed themselves automatically, thinking perhaps I was a priest, garbed for a swim, and as I went back to my car, I heard them banging around in their cabin, whooping like Indians.

"The worst is over," was a way of speaking. The "road" forded and reforded Coyote Creek (a lovely stream under other conditions), shelv-

33

ing high along the bank on one side and then the other, rain-pooled, rocky, ribbon-narrow, dropping me fast with thunder at my back, and the only good omen a flight of blue birds across the very hood of the car.

The canyon kept widening, however, and the flow of sweat had slackened, my muscles relaxed, and I came at last to an angel — a woman in a white dress who vanished into her cabin as I drove up. In the window was the face of her daughter, who spoke sweetly in the grave manner of the country, when I asked her where I was.

"Guadalupita Valley," she said, "You bring rain with you. Gracias, señor."

"The road is better?"

"Truly a fine road hereafter."

"Thank you, thank you!" I said, as if she were personally responsible for this engineering miracle.

The rain caught up with me as I reached Guadalupita store and stopped to drink a cold bottle of soda pop, utterly relaxed as the fall turned to hail, then back to rain and finally to drip, cool on my hot skin. I snapped on the car radio and it crackled hopelessly with static.

The valley continued to widen as I neared Mora. West northwest the triple peaks of Truchas formed the horizon. Beyond the eastern hills lay plains and rivers, the Ozarks, the Appalachians — pallid country, all of it. My compass swung west southwest.

I had not liked Mora on my first visit, and I

34

liked it even less this time, sensing there a focus of evil forces, personified by a horseman leading another horse, an Anglo of such de-bauched visage as to chill my blood.

Rolling down the road to Vegas I had an ex-citing glimpse of an all but naked girl in a road-side *acéquia*, and I thought of Frank Waters's *People of the Valley*, laid in this very region, with its beautiful episode of María and the sol-dier at the pool; and I was uncertain as to which is the more memorable and lasting, lit-erature or life.

Flying back to Albuquerque from Los Alamos in a Carco Beechcraft, I experienced a feeling of flight not possible in a large plane. We blew off The Hill's landing strip like a leaf in the wind, and floated out over the valley of the Rio Grande, as the mesa fell away steeply beneath us. I sat alongside the pilot, three other passen-gers in the seat behind us, and he pointed out the pueblos as we passed over them, following the serpentine source of life, matrix of New Mexican history and culture, fed by snow and spring, the grand configuration now visible in a glance, comprehensible in its symbiotic parts.

Rain and the Beechcraft fell together on the airport at Albuquerque, and I stood around on the edge of the cool curtain while waiting for a westbound plane. Belted down in TWA's Flight 82, then circling north over the city, I had a last sight of the Sandías and a final good omen, not one but two perfect rainbows — *circo iris, arco-*

35

baleno, arc-en-ciel, regenbogen, rainbow, take your choice, all beautiful, all blessed — arching from Bernalillo to where Highway 66 breached the range.

It was a turbulent flight, too rough to serve food and drink, and I buckled down and read the society page of the *Santa Fe New Mexican*, able to absorb only the frothiest of prose.

Phoenix was hot, windy, sandy. I stayed belted in the plane.

Approaching the Colorado, we overtook the high brown front of the sandstorm, and then saw the river at Blythe, looking like silver on the dark body of the earth, while the western sky gave the day angry ending, symbolic of the struggle between the states for the Southwest's most precious element. The land beneath me was California.

3

THE SOUTHWEST:
AN ESSAY ON THE LAND

Start with the land. It was here first and it will be here last. I have called it a great dry and wrinkled land. Those are the basic characteristics of the Southwest. Climate and configuration. Absence of abundant rainfall. Vastness of mountains, deserts, and distance under the clear skies. Add color, and an abiding Indo-Hispano influence.

Although some find it hard to delimit the Southwest — how far northeast does it go? — it is easy to recognize. *Sun, silence, and adobe* is how Charles F. Lummis characterized it. He was its first booster, a tough little Yankee who came in the 1880s walking all the way and writing letters ahead to the *Los Angeles Times*. It was he who gave the Southwest its generic name.

There are two kinds of Southwesterners: native and adopted. The former were here first — Pimas and Papagos, Yumas, Apaches and Navajos, to name the chief tribes. They or their forebears were here as long as 15,000 years ago, and their descendants will probably be here after Anglos have run out of energy and means to live in cool and mobile comfort.

Adopted Southwesterners like Lummis can't

contain the joy with which the Southwest fills them. Their enthusiasm attracts immigrants. In our time the Southwest is suffering rapid change. Coal-burning power plants multiply and the Four Corners grow dingy. The Grand Canyon is overrun by motorized rafters and transisterites. Our lust for energy dams the rivers. Missile sites, bombing ranges, nuclear testing, and mock desert warfare, all disturb Lummis's classic Southwest. When blowing dust annoys the urbanites, their reaction is to blacktop the desert.

It is a fragile land of an interconnected ecology. The paucity of rainfall creates a delicate balance now threatened by man's thoughtlessness. Yet no culture lasts forever. Like its predecessors — Anasazi, Salado, Hohokam, Mimbres — our urbo-agri-industrial culture too will pass. To understand history is to concede that all cultures end. The poet writes, "The wave falls and the hand falls; thou shalt not always walk in the sun." Our time will probably last longer than any thus far because we are a clever technical people. If we can learn to exploit the sun's energy, we might live by its heat and light for many millennia — but even then not forever, for the sun's life also is limited.

There is a new desire to control the growth we call Progress. The apple ripens, man eats it. The law of growth and hunger. Because the Southwest is enormously beautiful and its climate mostly moderate, people will continue to come to it.

Yet the many changes it undergoes at men's hands will be on the surface. Although the land will be bulldozed, dug up, and pushed around, only a fraction of it will be disturbed. The Southwest is vast. Go on foot as Lummis did in 1884 or as Van Dyke did in 1900, and you will see its varied extent. To run the river on a raft is not to see much. Flying over the Southwest can be a good geography lesson. From the air can be seen why man went where he did, through passes and along river valleys. Man goes where water flows.

On my wall are colored references to this configured Southwest. They are three-dimensional maps of the component states that show how the land has determined history.

"In Nueva Granada the land is still supreme," Paul Horgan wrote of the Southwest, and went on to a lyrical description of the colored earth of New Mexico and Arizona, the region I like to call the Heart of the Southwest. "By land," explained Mary Austin, "I mean all those things common to a given region; the flow of prevailing winds, the succession of vegetal cover, the legend of ancient life; and the scene, above everything the magnificently shaped and colored scene." *Sky Determines* is the title and thesis of Ross Calvin's classic book about the Southwest's heavenly weather.

Where is the heart of hearts, the *cor cordium*? I keep moving it around. There are several places throughout the Southwest where it seems that all the power and glory of the world streams through me from the earth back to the sun and where I feel like a channel in which truth and beauty flow.

Mystical? Yes. The Indians have long harmonized with the mysteries of the land. Their mountains were the homes of the gods. As the Greeks deified Olympus, so do the Navajos revere their sacred peaks. The Papagos of southwestern Arizona look up to the peak of Baboquívari where the gods rule the elements.

Why do I write again about the Southwest? Because I love the land and write from love undertoned by lament. Its immigrants are often spoilers, dependent upon machines for their needs and comforts. Their cities grow like cancers. Their urban towers, incongruous *casas grandes*, could have been erected anywhere in the world. Their cities' streets are impacted with traffic, the skies obscured, the days and nights grown noisy. *Sun, silence, and adobe* are unknown to inhabitants of the concrete.

I am content to live out my life on the *bajada* of the Santa Catalinas, facing south to the mountains of Mexico. Do I proclaim Tucson to be the heart of hearts? It is obviously not the geographical heart, nor is it the spiritual center, which some say is at Oraibi, Shiprock, or Taos Pueblo. Tucson is to me the intellectual heart and I dwell on its slope because the Southwest's major university and research library are nearby. As a writer, my roots are nourished by the records of the past as well as by the beauty of the present.

Thus I live on the edge of the Old Pueblo, a community founded the year before the signing of the Declaration of Independence. The only competitor for my residential affection is that even older pueblo of Santa Fe. If the City of the Holy Faith had intellectual facilities to equal Tucson's, I could happily live there in the lee of the Sangre de Cristos.

This river-bounded domain of southern Arizona and northern Sonora is the old Pimería Alta — the Land of the Upper Pimas — first civilized by Padre Eusebio Kino, a German-educated Italian who came from Spain in 1687 as a Jesuit missionary, bringing livestock, fruits, and grains to trade for Indian souls. Kino was the first creative Southwesterner and he remains one of the greatest. Although he did not build the Mission San Xavier del Bac in the form we know today, he did found the mission to honor St. Francis Xavier, there on the western bank of the Rio Santa Cruz, at the site of the Papago village of Bac.

Many descriptions of San Xavier have been written by travelers during the past two centuries. None is more glowing than that by the late Nancy Newhall, in a monograph with eloquent photography by Ansel Adams. High Mass moved her to this passage:

"Here the Mission is crowded with a barbarian dusk and shot with startling splendor. Dark massive faces of Papago women under silk kerchiefs of turquoise, emerald, purple. A Mexican beauty in tangerine, with a gold scarf over her head. A little Papago girl with a crown of scarlet poppies on her jet pigtails. Old Papago men in blue jeans, with wide straw hats in their huge hands and silver buckles under their paunches. Yaqui patriarchs, of immense dignity, with long braids tied around their heads with ribbon. A Mexican baby, with a skin like dark cream, in a cloud of a pink dress caught here and there with forget-me-nots. And old women, Mexican and Indian, with their heads draped in black lace mantillas, the lace often hanging down over rough old sweaters or house-dresses pale with washing.

"Black-headed babies squall or crow, resisting every effort to hush them. A dog or two wanders in through the open doors, sometimes joining with wagging tail a solemn procession down the aisle. Little Papago acolytes shake their scarlet skirts at him and urge him off with a surreptitious foot, usually in vain. It does not matter; nothing mars the great prayer of the Mass.

"Overhead, serene and luminous, rise the arches and the domes. And now the celestial court — the angels, the flying cherubim, the saints appearing in their niches, the Mother and Son — seem strange no longer. They have become one indivisible universe with their worshippers, their rich setting no more bizarre than this their congregation.

"Out in the sun again, the dark faces and the gemlike colors are seen to be native to the

42

desert plain, the sharp peaks, the immense horizons."

Last Christmas Eve I attended midnight Mass at San Xavier. The floodlit mission, visible from afar, was truly the White Dove of the Desert. By eleven o'clock the nave and transept were crowded, and I stood against the wall by the crèche. Since this is the mission church of San Xavier Reservation, most of the celebrants were Papagos. The red-robed acolytes' round brown faces shone with mingled awe and mischief as they tended the priest while he placed the babe in the hammock of the crèche.

All were transfixed. Smoke from the priest's censer rose to the arches and the painted vault of the roof. The choir sang in unison. The bread was broken, the wine drunk. As lips touched and hands clasped, a wave of love surged through the church. It was Epiphany, as Christ spoke with the inner voice.

The church emptied into the night. Frost had begun to form. The bittersweet smell of burning mesquite filled the air. A half moon rose over the hill. The celebrants went their ways into desert and town.

How should one first come to the Southwest? There are various ways, all beautiful, some more dramatic. The southern routes are the subtlest. There the plains of Texas and Oklahoma merge with those of New Mexico. Between the pages of one of my books is pressed a florarium of Highway 54, fragile evidence that all the flowers of summer once lit this way southwest.

If one comes by Roswell on the Pecos, one finds Paul Horgan-Peter Hurd country. Their stories and paintings were created here. The road tracks northwest across grasslands and up Hondo Creek into the Sacramentos, past San Patricio where Peter Hurd now lives. Then it crosses the Mescalero Apache reservation and drops into the Tularosa basin, a *bolsón* or pocket between the Sacramento and the San Andrés ranges.

Hurd and Horgan celebrated those lands east of the mountains; Tularosa is the domain of Eugene Manlove Rhodes, the only rangeland peer of Arizona's Ross Santee — both men with power over cattle, horses, and words. Rhodes lies buried high in the San Andrés mountains. The road to his grave crosses the White Sands, now a missile range closed to public access.

Trinity Site is nearby, where The Bomb was first exploded. Man's compulsion to create and destroy distinguishes this place. Over it rises Sierra Blanca, high landmark of southeastern New Mexico. On its shoulder is the village of Cloudcroft, as poetically named as Arizona's Snowflake (the charm of which is somewhat lessened when we know that it was named for two worthy Mormons, Mr. Snow and Mr. Flake).

Rhodes's pocket empties into Texas's outpost of El Paso. Three Texans glorify that city — Hertzog the printer, Lea the writer-painter, and Cisneros the illustrator. No other south-

44

western city can boast such a creative trio. Their collaboration somewhat gentles this rough Texan counterpart of Albuquerque and Phoenix.

The mountains of southern Arizona hardly rival the Rockies. The sandy wastes of the southwestern corner are beautiful only to a viewer with time and lenses to look at them long and lovingly as Joseph Wood Krutch did. In the final twenty years of his life, that transplanted philosopher-naturalist was the most eloquent spokesman for the Southwest.

South from Willcox the road runs to the Mexican border. To the west lies a *playa* that rainfall turns into a shallow lake. To the east are the Chiricahuas, the former domain of Cochise and his Apache raiders. It is a lonely road. Few travel this route to the twin border cities of Douglas and Agua Prieta. All the land of southern Arizona rises gradually from the Gila River valley. Sage and juniper yield to grama grass and oak. Cattle fatten on a range enriched by the rainy seasons of summer and winter.

The high stack of the smelter heralds the company town of Douglas, where coffee may be taken at the opulent Gadsden Hotel. Beyond in Bisbee, the Lavender Pit could have served Doré as a coppery model for his hellish drawings. The old Copper Queen Hotel offers hospitality, although Bisbee suffers from a dwindling supply of profitable ore.

The road leads back to Tucson through Tombstone on its high mesquite mesa and over the grasslands and oak groves which lie between the Whetstones and the Santa Ritas. This is an Arizona without the dramatic appeal of the Painted Desert or the Grand Canyon; it is a grassy land of peace and plenty.

The northern ways are more thrilling. They come through the passes of Ratón and Wolf Creek. The former is the old Santa Fe Trail that led from the Missouri frontier by Las Vegas to the City of the Holy Faith. At trail's end is piñon and juniper country where the earth is reddish, the vegetation dark green. It was near here at Laguna that Haniel Long, the sage of Santa Fe, first came under the spell of the Southwest.

"I stepped down into the freshness and vastness of the diminutive piñon forest," he recalled, "and as I walked about among the blue-green odorous trees, I felt like a giant, for over their heads was the horizon of the mountains. On a nearby hill was the ancient town, the first pueblo I had ever seen. I was pleased that houses could be so unpretentious, built simply of the earth and leaving nothing to be improved upon. So with the little trees: they gave me the pleasure that comes of small perfect things which adapt their forces without scattering or waste."

Coming east from California, the dramatic route is over the Sierra Nevada via Tioga Pass and the abrupt drop into the Owens River valley. Ansel Adams photographed these mountains and this valley for an edition of Mary Austin's *The Land of Little Rain*. It is a land akin to northern New Mexico, and the Sierra Nevada is a big brother to the Sangre de Cristo. The valley's villain is Los Angeles, which bought up the land and aqueducted its water. In her outrage, Mary Austin foretold doom for the Angel City. She probably meant earthquake and fire. Having covered the destruction of San Francisco in 1906 for Lummis's *Out West*, she knew what can happen to a city when the earth shakes and burns. Now Los Angeles's end may come from overpopulation, industrialization, and pollution. Choking and smothering also spell doom.

From Owens River valley the road crosses the Panamints and Death Valley, through lands of less than little rain. The first collaboration between Ansel Adams and Nancy Newhall produced a beautiful book on Death Valley. The sculptor Gordon Newell lives in the Panamints with stone for his chisel and unlimited crystal air of a clean world. "When you tell about this beautiful part of the Southwest," he wrote me, "consider the thought that 'Death Valley' is a misnomer, for that is where Life best demonstrates its ability to survive. From pupfish to creosote, a continuity persists that belies the name 'Death.' That a few confused tourists left their bones there is pretty irrelevant in the scale and scheme of time and weather."

Where Utah yields the Strip to Arizona, the land rises onto the forested Kaibab plateau to end at the North Rim of the Grand Canyon.

Although it is only a dozen miles across, by car it takes hours to drive the two hundred miles around this deep wound in the earth's body.

I was on the South Rim at Christmastime. Snow shrouded the canyon as I walked along the edge at twilight in a thin fall of flakes. Sweet chimney smoke filled the air, and that smell of burning pinewood recalled my childhood transits of territory when the incense of sawmill meant that California came on the morrow.

A darkened building proved to be the studio of the Kolb brothers, the early river-runners and photographers. There on display was the very boat that had carried them through the Grand Canyon from Wyoming to Mexico. Ellsworth Kolb's book of their adventure was my first Southwest book. It was a gift from my father on my fifteenth birthday, a few months before his early death. I have kept it all these years as a talisman.

There are other gifts that I cherish from my father's travels in the Southwest. One is an Apache basket that he bought at the Fred Harvey shop in The Alvarado at Albuquerque. Before that beautiful hotel was bulldozed for a parking lot, I often went there to watch the passing trains. Albuquerqueans were wont to set their watches by those Santa Fe trains: *California Limited, Scout, Missionary, Navajo, Chief, Super Chief,* and *El Capitan.* Once when speaking to a conference at The Alvarado, I paused upon hearing the sigh of relaxing Westinghouses. "What train is that?" I asked the chairman. He pulled out his watch. "Eastbound mail," he said. I resumed my talk.

I have taken my place in the company of travelers in the Southwest, and I go with their books in my baggage and their ghosts at my side. They are friendly ghosts. Some are heroic, more are obscure. First came Don Francisco Vásquez de Coronado. Although he did not find the Golden Cities of Cíbola (they proved to be the adobe pueblos of the Zuñi Indians), Coronado surely had a great trip. If there was no poetry in him when in 1540 he and his men marched up the valley of the San Pedro, deep into Arizona and New Mexico and as far as the present-day Nebraska, was he indifferent to the sky's blueness and its glitter at night? To his dying day did he not remember the smell of mesquite with which his men made their fires? Four hundred and thirty-six years later, the valley of the San Pedro is still thicketed with huge mesquites. If Coronado came for gold and Kino for God, now in our time the poet and the photographer come for the glory of form and color of earth and sky.

Earlier in that same century the mystical healer Alvar Nuñez Cabeza de Vaca also came this way, one of the last survivors of a ship-wreck on the Florida coast. It took those wanderers eight years to cross the continent, during which they discovered they had the power to heal the sick. If I were to choose a single masterpiece of Southwest literature it might be

49

Haniel Long's *Interlinear to Cabeza de Vaca*, a prose poem that extracts the inner meaning of the Spaniards' odyssey. "Crack the rock if so you list," wrote another poet, "bring to light the amethyst." This Long did in his jewel of a book.

In later centuries there came the Jesuit Kino, and Anza, the Sonoran commander, and Garcés, the Franciscan priest. It was Garcés who crept to the bottom of the Grand Canyon and in 1776 rode his mule into Oraibi on that fateful fourth day of July. He was turned away by the Hopis. They preferred their gods to his.

My roll call of heroes includes Kearny, who seized the Southwest from Mexico; Cooke, who blazed the first wagon road to the Pacific; and the Apache chiefs Mangas Coloradas and Cochise, fighters to hold their domain. "I think continually of those who were truly great," wrote Stephen Spender; and as I travel in the Southwest, I repeople it with its heroic leaders. With them at my side, I am never alone nor lonely.

West-southwest of Tucson, the Papaguería yields to Sonora. This is still the domain of Padre Kino, although three centuries have passed since he came this way on foot and horseback, setting records of endurance that have never been equaled. The Papagos are a solid race whose bulk conceals their poetic legendry. "People of the Crimson Evening," they have been called. Their land was not coveted by conquistadors, missionaries, gold seekers, or settlers.

50

"So the Papagos wandered, calm and smiling, back and forth across the waste of brilliant barrenness," wrote anthropologist Ruth Underhill. "They shot the ground squirrels and the rats and birds. They picked the caterpillars from the bushes. They shook the seeds from every blade of wild grass. They brushed the spines from cactus stems and roasted them for hours in a pit with a fire over it. I have never heard one of them object to this plan of life. Rather, an old woman telling me of it sighed and said: 'To you Whites, Elder Brother gave wheat and peaches and grapes. To us, he gave the wild seeds and the cactus. Those are the *good* foods,' "

The peak of Baboquívari rises above the desert floor to visibility for a hundred miles around. At the other end of the range stands Kitt Peak, upon which astronomers have built a great national observatory. "Men with Long Eyes," the Papagos call them. In granting the scientists rights on their mountain, the Indians retained those to the native wood — the slow-burning, gray-barked Arizona oak, *Quercus Arizonica Sargent.*

There are many devices on Kitt Peak whereby astronomers scan the sky. I leave them to their devices. When I go up the mountain, it is to picnic among the jay-haunted oaks. In the summertime the air is cool up there. The ground is strewn with tiny acorns. I once saw children gathering them, and this dialogue took place:

51

"What are you going to do with those acorns?" I asked.

"Sell them to neighborhood children."

"For how much?"

"A penny a handful."

"May I buy some?"

The children thought a minute and then one said, "No."

"Why not?"

"Your hands are too big."

Arizona and New Mexico display great cultural differences. The former is Indo-Anglo, the latter Indo-Hispano. The reason is a river and its valley, the Rio Grande, New Mexico's great river along which Indians, Spaniards, and Mexicans have acculturated for a thousand years.

The continuity of life along the Rio Grande and its tributaries gave New Mexico a richness not present in any other part of the Southwest. That culture endures to this day. There are eighteen hundred miles of river from Boca del Rio, where the Rio Grande debouches into the Gulf of Mexico, to its source in the Colorado Rockies.

I know the Rio Grande only from the point in Texas where the Pecos flows into the greater river; and I know it best between Albuquerque and where the river engorged itself into the volcanic plain. From there I take off on roads high into the ranges on either side.

History has touched this valley long and

lightly. Like the Papaguería, it was never raped. No desirable metals were unearthed there. Water is the only precious element. The Rio Grande is a perennial stream, fed by the eternal snows and springs of the San Juan Rockies. In spring the river's course is green, in autumn gold, in winter bare. Cottonwoods are the predominant trees. In his history of the Rio Grande, Paul Horgan writes lyrically of the cottonwood:

"Its wood was soft and manageable, and it supplied material for many objects. Its silver bark, its big, varnished leaves sparkling in the light of summer and making caverns of shade along the banks, its winter-hold of leaves the color of beaten thin gold lasting in gorgeous bounty until the new catkins of spring — all added grace to the pueblo world. The columnar trunks were used to make tall drums, hollowed out and resonated with skins stretched over the open ends. The wood was hot fuel, fast-burning, leaving a pale, rich ash of many uses. Even the catkins had personal use — eaten raw, they were a bitter delicacy in some towns. And in that arid land, any tree, much less a scattered few, or a bounteous grove, meant good things — water somewhere near, and shade and shelter from the beating sun and talk from trifling leaves."

The Indian pueblos line the river from Isleta to Taos. The latter had to leave the gorge to find its water along a tributary. At Cochití Pueblo the Jémez range forms the western wall. A rocky road climbs to the plateau from juniper through piñon and ponderosa to aspen and spruce. It is a steep road, patrolled by squirrels and bluejays. History has overlooked this lonely canyon.

The road leads to a place where history came with terrible impact: the Los Alamos laboratories of the Atomic Energy Commission. Here The Bomb was built. The shock waves from its detonation are still traveling.

The road down from the Pajarito plateau crosses the river at Otowi. There during the war, Edith Warner and an Indian from the nearby pueblo of San Ildefonso had a tearoom to which the scientists came for relaxation. She knew that it was a holy place. The presence of water in an arid land — a river, a spring, a fountain, or an oasis — means that the gods are near. "This morning I stood on the river bank to pray," Peggy Pond Church quotes Edith Warner in *The House at Otowi Bridge*, tenderest of Southwest classics. "I knew then that the ancient ones were wise to pray for peace and beauty and not for specific gifts, except fertility which is continued life."

What a strange conjunction is that of Los Alamos and San Ildefonso, of laboratory and pueblo! The latter is an idyllic place of dusty plaza, kiva, and cottonwood. It is the home of Maria the potter, who lived on into her nineties. Nearby are the candlemakers called the Wicked

Wicks. With that many candles to burn, who would begrudge a burner at both ends?

The road back to Santa Fe passes the outdoor opera theater. There I was so bemused one summer by the soaring ecstasy of *Der Rosenkavalier* that I had almost to be helped to my car by a sweet usher from Española. There during the entr'acte may be seen a fashion show of capes and cloaks, of silks and corduroys, in all the colors worn by cloth. Chromatics to match the music.

In Santa Fe, bronze plaques commemorate Stravinsky's presence in the 1960s when his Mass was sung in the cathedral — Archbishop Lamy's cathedral of St. Francis. When the first traders came in the 1820s, they found no trees to shade the dusty lanes and bare plaza. In *Commerce of the Prairies*, Gregg described Santa Fe as a huddle of mud houses, hardly the New Jerusalem.

Today, the city is a green park, guarded by the Sangre de Cristo range, the final thrust of the Rockies. Quaking aspens band the conifered mountainside, a stand that established itself where a fire once burned the evergreens. The leaves of *Populus tremuloides* are never still. They tremble even when there seems to be no movement of the air.

The road to Taos follows the river past orchards of apple and cherry, at last to gain the plain. The wise traveler pauses there to see a view like none other in the Southwest. It was D. H. Lawrence's favorite vista, across the gray-green sage — *Artemesia tridentata* — and golden-flowered rabbit brush to the blueness of Lobo Peak, Taos Mountain, and the gorge of the Rio Grande.

Taos was once the rendezvous of the trappers known as Mountain Men. In our time, poets, painters, photographers, and writers have been drawn there. Mabel Dodge and Tony Lujan, Mary Austin, Willa Cather, Frank Applegate, Edward Weston, and Ansel Adams are among those who have come and gone.

It was at Taos and Santa Fe that Ansel Adams first saw the Southwest. The time was the spring of 1927. By a coincidence, it was the very season and year that I first came to the Southwest — to the Old Pueblo of Tucson. His visit resulted in a Grabhorn Press book now of legendary rarity. It includes Ansel Adam's photographs and Mary Austin's essay on Taos Pueblo. Genius has never been more happily wed. Nowhere else did she write prose of such precise and poetical authority.

"Always for the most casual visitor at Taos, there is the appeal of strangeness; the dark people, the alien dress, the great house-heaps intricately blocked in squares of shadow and sunlight on tawny earthen walls." And then follows a calendar of seasonal vegetation. "Thickets of wild plums abound there, tangles of virgin's bower, meadow sweet, wild iris, blue bush lupins, and tufted grass. It is the wild plums that continue the note of aliveness, the sense of things going on, of contriving, which

56

is so characteristic of the Taos Valley scene." And so on through summer, fall, and winter. Their *Taos Pueblo* is a true and beautiful book by two consummate artists.

Now, half a century later, Taos teems with tourists in summer and skiers in winter. They trail fumes and leave their eternal litter. "Who killed Taos?" "I," said Cock Car, "I killed Taos with my internal combustion engine."

There is a long way back to Santa Fe. It heads north to Questa, then ascends the Red River (the little Red) past the molybdenum mine and over the pass in the lee of Mount Wheeler, New Mexico's highest point, to Eagle Nest Lake, Guadalupita, and Mora (all deep Penitente country) and down to Las Vegas and La Galeria de los Artesanos on the plaza in Old Town, a charming shop of books and crafts. The region's master novelist is Frank Waters. The Taos Indian mystique is the theme of *The Man Who Killed the Deer*, while in *People of the Valley*, Waters tenderly delineates the Hispano mores.

Here at Las Vegas, Kearny seized the Southwest for the United States when Governor Armijo prudently gave up without a fight. The Santa Fe Trail is now Interstate 25, and it follows the railroad known as Amtrak. I prefer to call it the Atchison, Topeka and Santa Fe, and I still think of its somewhat less than crack train as the *Super Chief*. Over these rails I first came west at the age of four months to seek my fortune.

57

Ribera is the double-tracked midpoint between Chicago and Los Angeles where the east-west trains meet. First one hears the growl of approaching Diesels. The eastbound's is deeper because the grade is rising toward Ratón. Then the opposing trains appear. Capped and gloved on their thrones, the engineers salute. Porters lean from open vestibules and trade fond obscenities. Passengers are unaware of the encounter. I alone witness that orgasmic meeting of the silvery trains.

If history has been gentle to the Rio Grande's valley, the tributaries and uplands have not been touched at all. Above Española, life goes on as it has for centuries. Cottonwoods change their leaves with the seasons. Cherries flower and fruit and go bare. Apples ripen and fall. Red peppers hang in strings, then are ground into fiery powder. The houses of stone or adobe have steep roofs for snow to slide off. Piñon smoke sweetens the air. Although not the heart of the wide Southwest, this is surely New Mexico's heartland. If Coronado, Oñate, or Vargas came this way as they did so long ago, they would again call it New Spain, so much does it resemble the land of the mother country.

My destination is the Santuario of Chimayó, a primitive chapel with a healing shrine. Votive offerings and discarded crutches bear witness to pilgrims' faith. Two cottonwoods once guarded the sanctuary. Now only one remains, watered by an *acéquia* that flows past its base.

The stump of the other could serve as a picnic table for the weary suppliant.

From Chimayó the road climbs barren hills to the hogback village of Truchas, the Trout. Here in the high foothills of the Sangre de Cristos the roofs have an even steeper pitch. In the east rise the peaks of Truchas, second highest mountain in New Mexico. Beyond is the Pecos wilderness, fairest of Southwest uplands.

I have friends in Truchas, a mother and son who are the third and fourth generation of weavers. Her grandfather taught her to spin and weave in their natal village of Córdova. The mother's fingers are nimbler, the son's legs stronger as he dances on the treadle. In early autumn the shop is sun-warmed, while through the open window smoke drifts from cooking fires. Piñon, of course. Piles of it are stacked throughout the village. The peaks of Truchas rise heavenward. Here the universe stands still.

Is this journey's end? No, I have one more village to visit. Trampas, the Traps. Beavers were once taken here, hence the name. A small plaza, a little church whose bells have been removed for safekeeping. The one called Grácia (from its sweet tone) I once made ring with a rap of my knuckles. Good works were done here by Anglo architects. Nathanael Owings kept a road-widening from threatening the chapel; John Gaw Meem mercifully restored the towers.

On the edge of the village is a little master-piece of hydraulic engineering — a *canoa*, or canoe, made of hollowed out cottonwood logs. It carries water to the villagers' fields and orchards. I stop there to drink. A bluebird does the same.

"How old is that *canoa*?" I asked my friend Orlando from Nambé.

"Who knows?" the young Hispano replied. "My grandfather says his grandfather once helped replace the rotting logs. I think it is as old as Time itself."

From afar the Southwest appears even more enchantingly configured and colorful. At least it did to me during absence in New England. Winter was snowy, spring rainy, the summer humid. I longed for what, in his exile from New Mexico, Eugene Manlove Rhodes called "the glowing heart of the world."

And so I left Boston with no regret on the drive west-southwest. Each night holed up in a motel, I mapped the morrow's journey deeper into the heartland. In St. Louis I paused to see the fountain of fountains — Carl Milles's "The Meeting of the Waters," a great bronze group personifying the confluence of the Missouri and the Mississippi. There under a windy sky I spent an hour marveling at the lifesized figures of river god and goddess, tritons and naiads, fishes and shells — and getting soaked by the ever-shifting spray from the fountain's jets. Here was water to waste. Here the plenty of the country's greatest rivers makes water a common element. My thirst was for the arid lands where water is more precious than copper or gold.

From Denver I crossed South Park and ascended the Arkansas, climbed over Independence Pass and dropped down on Aspen, a mountain village that, like Taos, has suffered from pleasure seekers and the franchise wolves who come after them. I went on soon to Alamosa on the upper Rio Grande. Here the river is restrained by a weir to form a backwater for birds and boys with boats. On above, the stream narrows toward its source in the San Juans, flowing fast and tracking glitter in the early sunlight.

I climbed the road up South Fork, rising to the roar of white water and over Wolf Creek Pass and the continental divide where the view is far down on the first meander of the San Juan. To tarry there above tree line in summer is to call down the lightning, and so I switchbacked on to Pagosa Springs and on west to Durango and the Mesa Verde.

There at the matrix of Pueblo culture, I had reached the farthest north of my Southwest. Was it the prolonged drought of the thirteenth century that forced the dwellers to trek south to the Pajarito plateau and the Rio Grande and there re-establish their culture? No one knows for sure. On my first visit to the Mesa Verde many years before, I had a fleeting vision of the people of Spruce Tree House, climbing down the ladders and filing away, carrying little food and no water. I communed then with the mystique of the land. A beautiful expression of it is Mary Austin's *The Land of Journeys' Ending*, its prose lit by poetic insight as in this passage:

"Walking there, one of these wide-open summer days, when there comes a sudden silence, and in the midst of the silence a stir, look where you walk. If your feet stumble in a round depression, to the north of which you discover squarish, low mounds of reddish rock; if, beyond the margin of shallow basins, you observe windrows of loose stones pitched out from between the hills of corn long before the leveled space was taken by three-hundred-year-old pines, know that you are in the country of the Smallhouse People. Always incredibly, there lingers about these places, where once was man, some trace that the human sense responds to, never so sensitively as where it has lain mellowing through a thousand years of sun and silence."

The road leads south to Shiprock. Geologists call it a basalt plug. To the Navajos it was their salvation from the warlike Utes. When they sought refuge on it, the rock soared and bore them away to a safer land. No wonder they hold it sacred.

I passed Shiprock on the hundred-mile run to Gallup, that rough railroad town on the edge of the Navajo reservation. Here the Indian may be seen in the stages of disintegration — drinking, fighting, staggering, and falling to sidewalk and gutter. Here is the place to read *Laughing Boy*, La Farge's lament for a people debauched by an alien race. If the Navajos would recover their pride and become The Nation they call themselves, they should build a great wall between them and such towns.

My destination lay farther south at El Morro, the national monument called Inscription Rock, a buff-colored battlement of sandstone upon which passing travelers from the time of Don Juan de Oñate in 1605 have left their presence carved in the stone. *Pasó por aquí* — came this way — they declared. I once romantically proclaimed El Morro to be the Southwest's heart of hearts. Nowhere is there a better refuge from the threats of modern life. Few people go there. There are no lodgings, no concessions, nothing but a small museum and a vast sense of history. El Morro has been protected since President Theodore Roosevelt's time against all enemies save the wind and the rain.

Lummis photographed El Morro and called it The Great Stone Autograph Album. Mary Austin longed to be buried there. "Here at least I shall haunt," she wrote in *The Land of Journeys' Ending*, "and as the time-streams bend and swirl about the Rock, I shall see again all the times that I have loved, and know certainly all that I now guess at....You, of a hundred years from now, if when you visit the Rock, you see the cupped silken wings of the argemone

63

burst and float apart when there is no wind; or if, when all around is still, a sudden stir in the short-leaved pines, or fresh eagle feathers blown upon the shrine, that will be I, making known in such fashion as I may, the land's undying quality."

I have climbed to the top of El Morro and rested there with bluebird and butterfly and the shade of Mary Austin. Beyond to the east sits the old Acoma Pueblo, brooding, timeless; Zuñi lies to the west. It is land of beautiful choices.

"Water is what these Indians worship." Coronado reported to his viceroy, "because they say it is what makes the corn grow." The early Spaniards observed that the natives' worship included the offering of painted sticks, plumes, powders made of yellow flowers, and pieces of turquoise which were placed by springs.

The Indians still acknowledge the divinity of water. The Hopis employ serpentine rituals to call down the rain. The Papagos sing for power over the essential element.

Anglos also recognize water as the Southwest's basic element. Who owns water, owns all. They have made it serve us with dams and canals to create power and irrigate crops. Yet they waste water as if it were an inexhaustible resource. They fail to realize that there could come another drought such as the one that ended human life on the Mesa Verde.

The water gods must be propitiated. One way is for each community in the arid lands to dedicate a fountain to the divinity of water. Where water is abundant, as in St. Louis, a fountain is less meaningful, beyond the mere beauty of it, than a fountain where water is scarce. Southwesterners should be taught from childhood that the source of their water lies beyond the faucet.

I have gone time and again to the great river dams of the Southwest — to Laguna, Imperial, Hoover, and Glen Canyon on the Colorado; to Roosevelt on the Salt, Coolidge on the Gila, and to Elephant Butte on the Rio Grande. Only for two — Laguna and Roosevelt — do I have especial affection. Is it because they were the only ones known to my father? To them he made the hard journey by mule-drawn wagon that was necessary in 1909.

Laguna and Roosevelt were the first dams to be constructed under the Reclamation Act of 1902. Then a horticulturist in the United States Department of Agriculture, my father came from Washington to inspect these new sources of life and light and power.

Laguna Dam on the Colorado above Yuma was originally a mile-wide, Indian weir-type barrier of rock and brush, meant to restrain the river's spring flooding and to furnish water for crops on reclaimed desert land. Laguna was eventually made obsolete by nearby Imperial Dam.

I have gone there on the river in the blazing

heat of August. Now motorized campers abound. Few if any know the history and meaning of man's achievement in subduing the Colorado. None knows why I go there with thankful heart to honor my father and to marvel at the hydraulics. Sluiced water roars into the desilting basins and is canalled into the Imperial Valley of California to irrigate carrots, cotton, melons, and lettuce. Birds bob on the lake. Arrow weed and tules line the banks. The mountains look as if they had been cut out of cardboard. The air shimmers with heat.

East of Phoenix the road leads to the junction where the Apache Trail enters the domain of the Tonto Apaches. Men of that tribe were a main source of labor when Roosevelt Dam was built during the years 1905–1911. President Theodore Roosevelt himself, for whom it was named, dedicated the dam with a moving peroration:

"I do not know if it is of any consequence to a man whether he has a monument. I know it is of mighty little consequence whether he has a statue after he is dead. If there could be any monument which would appeal to any man, surely it is this. You could not have done anything which would have pleased and touched me more than to name this great dam, this great reservoir site, after me, and I thank you from my heart for having done so."

Then and now, Theodore Roosevelt Dam is the greatest masonry dam in the world, built of sandstone blocks quarried from the very walls of the canyon whose river, the Salt, is dammed. This majestic barrier has meant more to Arizona than any other single undertaking. By its mastery of the Salt and the lower Gila, the city of Phoenix and the surrounding Valley of the Sun were made to flourish and be fruitful.

I have gone there to Roosevelt Dam in all seasons. In winter the land is the most beautiful, its strong colors subdued and made restful to the eyes. Then are seen soft greens, browns, and blues under gray skies. The water behind the dam is then olive green instead of the blue of summer.

Coolidge Dam on the Gila lies southeast of Roosevelt Dam. It was built of concrete of an odd bulbous design. From a vantage point downstream, the dam's face is seen to be ornamented with great cement eagles. Green water from the penstocks streams languidly into the canyon that carries it through the mountains to the lower lands it irrigates.

Lake San Carlos is fed by the capricious Gila that rises in the wilderness of the Arizona — New Mexico boundary. When Coolidge Dam was dedicated in 1927, the water was very low, a circumstance that led Will Rogers to quip to President Coolidge, "If this was my lake, I'd mow it."

Few people go there except to fish in the lake. In summer the heat is fierce. Then the sotol sends up its golden-candled stalk. The Pinals dance in the sun. This is the land celebrated by Ross Santee — horse-wrangler, artist, writer, laureate of the Arizona range. On the slopes of the Pinaleños, his ashes were strewn.

Each of us seeks his state of grace. I have tendered here ways by which I have found mine. The Southwest has many hearts, synchronized by configuration and color. Even though we cannot define and delimit the Southwest to the satisfaction of all its lovers, we all know when we have reached it, whether it be west of the Pecos, south of the Mesa Verde, east of the Sierra Nevada and the Colorado, or north of the Sonoran rivers and the mountains of Chihuahua.

Salmon-colored cliffs, dove-colored deserts, rocky peaks and wooded ranges; hogans, wickiups, ramadas, and concrete towers; dust storms, flash floods, and red skies at morn and evening — nowhere do they come together with such beautiful meaning as they do in the Southwest.

Whose Southwest is it? Does it belong to the Indians? They were here first. Yet they were not always here. They too came from elsewhere, from South America or Asia. So did cattle, sheep, and horses. Then what *is* native? Ocotillo and saguaro. Copper, gold, and turquoise. The horned toad and the cactus wren and the rivers that run when the weather comes from off the ocean of storms.

The Papagos have always known from where the weather comes. In ancient times when they made their annual journey to the Pacific for salt, they sang this song:

By the sandy water I breathe in the smell of the
    sea,
From there the wind comes and blows over the
    world.
By the sandy shore I breathe in the smell of the
    sea,
From there the clouds come and rain falls over
    the world.

When one is far from the Southwest or when one is no longer able to roam, how can one best evoke the colored lands? Imagination serves. Photographs help. On walls at home one can see Shiprock at sunrise, the White Sands by moonlight, or the towers of the White Dove and the helmet of Baboquívari.

Maps lend the illusion of distance. There is a geological map of Arizona in pastel colors to delight as well as inform. And paintings that exalt our view of earth and sky. Maynard Dixon is my favorite painter of the Southwest. His technique was ever equal to his vision. He never stopped growing as an artist, so that the work of his old age was the most daring of all. Navajo painters portray horses as winged creatures of light. Painting is an act of worship and glorification.

There are simpler evocators of the Southwest. Copper lumps and chunks of turquoise.

Blue shells from the gulf and bits of petrified wood from the Painted Desert. White sands of gypsum trickling through the hourglass. Or a page from the Northland Press up in Coconino County.

Books are truly the Southwest's most magical surrogates. We have only to read them and be transported onto the continuum of history that carries us back to when man first entered this great old dry and wrinkled land.

Designed By Ward Ritchie

Composed by Typecraft, printed by Fabe
Litho, Tucson, and bound by Roswell Book
Binding, Phoenix.